Power

to

Heal

The mystical life
of
Emma Curtis Hopkins

Power to Heal

The mystical life
of
Emma Curtis Hopkins

Told by Ruth L Miller
Illustrated by Martha Shonkwiler

WiseWoman Press

Power to Heal: The mystical life of Emma Curtis Hopkins

Told by Ruth L Miller
Illustrated by Martha Shonkwiler

WiseWoman Press
Portland, Oregon, USA

ISBN: 978-0-945385-28-8

Printed in USA

Imagine...

Imagine being a girl whose father is fighting in the Civil War. You love to read and learn, but there's a lot of work to do to help your mother keep the farm and family together, so you dream a lot...

Imagine that when you grow up and marry, your husband and son become ill, a woman offers to help them get through an illness and they are healed—with no medications!

Imagine that you make up your mind to learn how to do this yourself, and do...

Imagine what you would do if you knew how to heal anyone of any illness or distress—wouldn't you want to share it with the world? Well that's exactly what Emma Hopkins did...

CONTENTS

Beginnings

She was born September 2, 1849, the first of nine children. She was named Josephine Emma Curtis.

Her parents owned a dairy farm near Killingly, Connecticut. Her father was a good farmer, and the family was quite comfortable.

Josephine Emma loved to read, but as the eldest daughter, she also spent many hours helping with the chores and caring for the other children. Each day started with helping with her younger brothers and sisters, helping put breakfast on the table, helping with cleaning the house, and getting everybody to school.

After school and on Sundays, though, she would play outside and let her imagination soar. At one point, she picked out a piece of land near the farm and began imagining a hospital there, where sick children whose family had no funds could be cared for.

Then, in 1861, the year Josephine turned twelve, the Civil War began. Her father did what almost every other man in the northern states did. He joined the Army to save the Union.

Like most of the men who fought in the War Between the States, her father thought he'd be back in a few months, but it was almost 4 years before he returned.

The war years were hard. Almost every man in town was in the Army and without them the work they usually did wasn't done as well, so farms didn't do very well. Then there was too little rain, so the some of the crops failed. On top of all that, many of the foods and tools produced by the women, children, and older men who stayed home were sent to the fighting armies.

So families had to go without a lot while their men were away. Sometimes they were very hungry, and often cold and tired.

Still, the children went to school, and the families went to church on Sundays, walking a mile or so each way.

It was probably on one of those walks home that Josephine Emma stopped by a gate in the early evening and saw a family sitting at dinner. Even though she herself was hungry, she felt an appreciation that it was possible for her neighbors to have their needs met.

As she turned back to the road home, she still felt that gratitude. And then, to her delightful surprise, just a few minutes later, someone offered her an abundant meal to share with her own family! In that moment, she learned something very important, but it was years before she figured out how that happened.

Time went by, and after four long years, when the War ended, the whole Curtis family was glad to have their father back.

But their happiness was not complete. They soon saw that he had been wounded, and most of his leg had been cut off to save his life.

Without that leg, he could no longer manage the farm on his own. The children still had to do most of the chores—almost as much as when he'd been gone!

As the eldest, Josephine Emma had helped her mother keep the farm going during the War, and helped care for her younger brothers and sisters, too. Now she helped her father until the younger children were big enough to manage the farm with him. It was difficult for them to grow enough to support the family and still have some to sell for cash to buy other supplies.

When he realized the problem, Mr. Curtis began to sell real estate to supplement the farm income.

He did well, and finally, Josephine Emma was freed from helping keep the farm and family together. She could read and study, and with her father's additional income, she could go to Academy!

She was admitted just before her 16th birthday, in 1865. There she dropped her first name and became known simply as "Emma."

Her love of reading paid off at the Academy. She shone as a student and helped in some of the classes. A year later, she had completed as many courses as women were allowed to then, and was graduated.

Emma was asked to teach in that very school the following fall. This was unusual in the mid-1800s; teaching was considered a man's job back then. But so many men had died during the War that few were available to fill the openings. So Emma was among the first young women to teach in a regular school. This helped establish today's tradition of women as teachers.

Miss Curtis, as her students called her, taught for several years and really enjoyed both learning and teaching. She taught mathematics, including geometry, as well as both ancient and modern literature.

Then, in 1873 or '74 (we're not sure when), she accepted a proposal from George Hopkins, an English teacher in the same school, and they were married during the summer of 1874.

Married women were not allowed to teach in school then, so Emma had to give up the work that she loved and stay at home, doing all the many things it took to keep a household going, in those days.

She cooked and cleaned and did the laundry and kept the garden going. Since there weren't any refrigerators, she would walk to the grocer and buy food, then to the butcher for meat almost every day. Then, in the evening, she would sew and mend and knit their clothes, while her husband would grade papers.

A year later they had a son, whom they named John Carver Hopkins. So, as many couples did at that time, Emma and her husband invited her youngest sister, Estelle, to live with them as a companion and helper.

The two women shared the chores, which took a long time in those days, with no washing machines, microwaves, or even electricity! Emma really appreciated her sister's help, and used the time that was freed to play with her son and keep up with her reading—especially the latest in the sciences, which she found fascinating.

George moved from teaching job to teaching job while he tried to earn enough money to pay off the loans he had taken to pay for college.

This meant they lived in small, rather poor homes in different parts of New England. Most of these houses were not very well built, and were often cold and drafty (no insulation back then!), but they had enough space for the couple, their son, and Emma's sister.

In those days, most streets were dirt. People rode horses or in horse-drawn carriages when they didn't walk or take the train. They heated their houses and ran their factories with wood or coal stoves, or open fireplaces, and at night they burned candles or oil lamps to see. To clean, they dusted, swept, and mopped in their houses, and rugs and blankets were taken outside to beat the dust out (there weren't any vacuum cleaners then, either!).

All this meant there was lots of dust and smoke in the air all the time, especially in towns and cities. Emma and her sister found that, with dirt everywhere, it was hard to stay healthy in those crowded little houses.

In fact, it seemed like every time there was a change in seasons, someone—or everyone!—in the house would get a cold, or worse.

Healing

Autumn of 1883 was the turning point for the Hopkins family.

That summer a neighbor had invited Emma to tea and introduced her to a famous teacher, Mrs. Mary Baker Eddy. During the afternoon, Mrs. Eddy had told the invited guests about the ideas that she had developed, which she called Christian Science. Mrs. Eddy said that her practice could replace traditional medicine and was a way for women to earn an income while providing a needed service in the community.

Emma, well-read in the sciences of the day, was not impressed. The human body, as she understood it, was a mechanical and chemical machine that needed mechanical and chemical treatment to be maintained or repaired. Prayer, she thought, could not possibly make a real difference.

That fall, however, her ideas were changed. Her little household was taken over by a "serious respiratory ailment" that no medical attention they could afford would help. So, with her neighbor's support and assistance, Emma tried Mrs. Eddy's approach. To her surprise and relief, she was immediately freed from her illness! Then, helped by her neighbor, she was able to bring her family safely through to even greater health than before.

Now Emma was impressed—this was something to learn more about! She made up her mind to study "at the source," with Mrs. Eddy in Boston.

At that time women had very limited rights. It was assumed that their men—father, husband, brother, or son—would take care of them in return for the housekeeping that women did. Few women were able to own property or even to earn a living outside the home. None could vote, and most were taught only enough to be able to read the Bible and count change for a purchase.

This meant that most women had no funds of their own, including Emma. And Emma's husband's income was not only limited but drained by the payment of his college debts. She didn't see how she could pay for the training she now so dearly wanted.

Finally, on December 12, she wrote a letter to Mrs. Eddy, requesting admission to her training course:

> I want to tell you that the beautiful theory you advanced has taken …so firm a hold on my heart … I am now anxious to learn more of the science … directly from your lips.

Requesting financial aid, she said, "I am happily married … my husband is deeply in debt … I cannot command a single dollar." Instead, she offered that Mrs. Eddy could "take all my first fees for … payment."

Mrs. Eddy agreed.

Emma was very excited and pleased. She persuaded her husband that she could help pay their bills with this new training, and he agreed. So, leaving her now school-age son at home with her younger sister and husband, she got on the stagecoach to Boston. And, for the next six weeks, she immersed herself in the basic practitioner's course at Mrs. Eddy's Massachusetts College of Metaphysics.

She completed the course on December 27, 1883. Her first opportunity to really apply her new skills came when her husband became seriously ill a few weeks later. With great determination and a lot of patience (and some help from her more practiced neighbor), she sat with him in prayer and treated his illness without medication. It worked.

Having proved herself and her method, Emma placed a business-card ad as a practitioner in Mrs. Eddy's magazine, called *The Christian Science Journal,* in February of 1884.

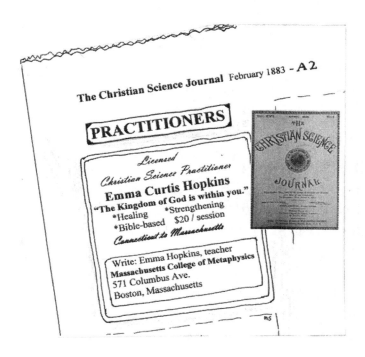

Emma's work as a practitioner was not always easy. She soon learned how important it was to bring her own thoughts and feelings in line if she was to help anyone else.

She later wrote about one experience during those early days (writing the way people did at that time, as if it were someone else having the experience):

There was a young practitioner who had spoken mighty praises in the morning of the way God, as the health and salvation of the people, would work through her to will and to do. She was not yet a successful healer and it troubled her. She acknowledged that God was doing great things through her and by her, even though she had not seen it so.

Her first case that morning was a lame man. She felt divine compassion for him, but had no thoughts, for she felt that if God did not manifest through her she could not make Him do so. And this held her silent, almost helpless, as if she were nothing at all and God were all.

All at once, quite unexpectedly to herself, she told the man to throw down his crutch and try to walk across the room. He obeyed at once. He found that he could limp without his crutch very well. She had him try two or three times more and he was cured.

It seemed as if his flesh and muscles drank in [the Spirit working though her]. Very likely he was thirsty for the waters of the refreshing God presence, with nobody's thought to interfere with him. (Lameness is a pretty sure sign of a mind interfered with.)[1]

But while healing others took effort in those first months, writing about ideas was easy.

Soon she was writing letters and short articles for the *Journal.* By fall of 1884, she was listed as the journal's editor and living part of each month in the dormitory of Mrs. Eddy's College of Metaphysics. So it appears that Emma worked off her tuition

[1] In *Scientific Christian Mental Practice,* Lesson Seven, p. 183 in the DeVorss edition. Also quoted in Miller's *Unveiling Your Hidden Power* (WiseWoman Press) Lesson Seven, p. 100.

for Mrs. Eddy that way, instead of paying her out of her practitioner's fees as they had originally agreed.

It was wonderful work for Emma, and she was good at it. She got to read and write and meet people who understood these new ideas. She pulled out her old Greek and Latin texts and found passages from thousands of years ago that supported these new ideas and explained how her family had been healed—and how she could do the same. She found newly translated texts from India and Persia and saw more support for these ideas. And, in addition to editing other peoples' articles and answering readers' questions, she wrote about her discoveries in her editorials.

Under her direction, the *Journal* grew in size, and was offered more regularly. Very soon, Mrs. Emma Curtis Hopkins was almost as well known to practitioners of Christian Science as was Mrs. Mary Baker Eddy.

A Sudden Change

In October of 1885, however, after months of riding the train and stage coach between her family's home in New Hampshire and Mrs. Eddy's Metaphysical College in Boston, Emma was fired—without any real explanation.

While some people accepted the possibility that funding was an issue, letters written in later years suggest that Emma's references to "other mystical writers" in her editorials, even though flattering to Mrs. Eddy, was unacceptable. After having explored a variety of teachings and seen her students lose their way, Mrs. Eddy held that there was one teacher of Christian Science and no others were worthy of mention—period.[2]

Although she'd been dismissed from her job, Emma always addressed Mrs. Eddy as her "dear teacher," calling herself "your devoted disciple" whenever she wrote to her. And, in spite of many criticisms from

---

[2] In those early years, Mrs. Eddy was discovering that people who learned her methods and modified them were not usually as effective as those who stuck to her teaching. As a result she became determined that all of her students would follow her method and no other.

Mrs. Eddy over the years, Emma always maintained her respect and gratitude. After all, Mrs. Eddy was the one who opened the doors for Emma to a universe of health and wellbeing!

In fact, Emma realized, it was essential to her own continued wellbeing and power as a healer that she give up any anger toward anyone, and focus on how much she appreciated all that Mrs. Eddy had done for her. She understood that we can't feel the power of the Holy Spirit when we're holding on to the idea that someone has hurt us.

We see a hint of her explanation for what happened in a letter she wrote in November of that year. In it, she said, "they could not understand my complicated way of explaining myself." And, in years to come, Emma's "sweet spirit of charity... with never a word of criticism of any sect or any school" would become a model for many.

A New Way of Life

Emma lost little time. She began at once to practice feeling the Holy Spirit at work in her life. She struggled at first, trying to understand just what had happened. It wasn't long, though, before she remembered what she had learned in her training: that God's good was to be found here, and she ought to have it.

Amazingly, she was almost immediately offered another job: taking over as interim editor for another magazine. It was based on the same principles she had learned to love with Mrs. Eddy, which was wonderful. The only hitch: it was published in Chicago.

But the job paid more than her husband's meager teaching salary, and it seemed like a great opportunity to try something new together. So George took a leave from his teaching position, expecting to return in the fall.

Then a woman she had met at Mrs. Eddy's college, Mary Plunkett, offered to help Emma use her teaching experience to offer classes on these new ideas in Chicago. Another wonderful opportunity!

So Emma and her family packed up, boarded a train, and moved from New England to the Midwest that winter.

And spring of 1886 found Mrs. Emma Hopkins in Chicago, with her husband, son, and sister, acting as interim editor of J. A. Swartz' *Mind Cure* magazine, while Mr. Swartz was on a trip to Europe.

For the next six months she worked hard to establish herself in this new city.

She not only edited the magazine. She also placed an ad in a Chicago paper offering to treat patients and inviting "a select few" to stay in her home for board and treatment. And, with Mary Plunkett, she opened the Emma Curtis Hopkins College of Christian Science.

At that time, Chicago was a booming transportation center, with rail, boat, and coach services from the Eastern states to the West, Midwest, and Northwest. People from all over Europe were immigrating to the northern Great Plains and Chicago was the transfer point for all freight and passengers seeking to "go West." Several newspapers served the city and a number of publishing houses offered books and magazines to the surrounding areas. Also, there was a variety of metaphysical and spiritualist associations scattered among the many Protestant churches and Catholic missions.

Emma followed her teacher's lead by making good use of the media. During the months she served as interim editor of *Mind Cure,* she reached out to some of the contacts she'd made as the editor of the *Christian Science Journal* and let them know about the change. She continued to advertise in the local papers for her classes and healing sessions. She even wrote

regular articles for one of the local papers—
which, in the years to follow, became a
weekly series of "Bible Lessons," which the
paper gladly printed.

As her name became known in the city,
Emma was asked to give regular public
lectures, in addition to the classes she
offered through the Seminary.

Finally, she and Mary Plunkett started what they called Hopkins Associations, with chapters around the country, made up of graduates of their classes (and the students of those graduates). To keep them informed, they sent a regular newsletter, with Emma's letters and articles, to the members of those chapters.

At first they all rented a small house in central Chicago, but after a year, things were going so well that they bought a large home with space for meetings and for faculty, clients, and even students to stay. Emma and her family were beginning to feel the true power of her teachings.

In fact, she was invited to Boston that fall to a meeting of independent teachers of "mental science" and was introduced there by a local physician as the "star that rose in the East and has spread its glory throughout the West." She went on from that meeting to teach a large class in New York City. She very much enjoyed that trip; it was a visit that would set the stage for her life some years into the future.

Starting Again

In 1888, however, things changed again. As she put it in later years, she had reached a new level in her understanding so "the world came unglued."

That spring, Mary Plunkett suddenly returned to New York, where, by the summer, she had built a rival school and association. On top of that, Mary took their newsletter and its mailing lists with her, leaving Emma again without an easy way to reach her audience.

Then there were problems among the staff at the school. Emma was a wonderful teacher, but she didn't like to run things, so people who worked for or volunteered at her school often went off on their own, and sometimes feelings were hurt in the process.

On top of all that, Emma's husband and son returned to George's family home in New England. They told her they simply were not happy in Chicago. George returned to his teaching position in New Hampshire and their son went to sea soon after. Emma felt she couldn't go with them.

That summer was very hard for her, and she tried not to feel abandoned.

She decided to focus on feeling the presence of God's Good. She knew this was her life's work, but she was still trying to discover what this new power truly was. She was sure God was the most important Presence in her life and that she was to share the gifts and understandings given to her. The question was, how?

So she prayed. She spent several days doing nothing but "practicing the Presence," and as she did so, a plan began to emerge.

Emma started to reorganize her life and work. Once more, she put an ad in the paper inviting patients into her home, as she had when they first came to Chicago. She arranged, again, to give lectures in libraries and meetings as a way to reach new potential clients and students. Then she talked to some of her advanced students and supporters and, together, they came up with a way to rebuild.

Her first step was to print up the notes from her beginning class and sell copies of them to all the students and graduates she could reach. That would raise some funds and give her an income. They called it *Class Lessons.*[3]

---

[3] These notes are now published as *Class Lessons of 1888* by WiseWoman Press.

Then they set about creating an officially recognized seminary, authorized by the state of Illinois, with a board and faculty made up of former students and clients. Some of them were ministers from local churches and some were former housewives who, like herself, had been trained as teachers and were lit with the fire of the Spirit.

Over a dozen people were on the faculty of the new Seminary, and they published their own journal. It was very successful, too: in the first five years, they graduated 350 people.

At one of those graduations, Emma stood up and told her students that "the world is their church," and they were to meet the needs of all people who were living "under the shadow of the mistaken needs of the past." She told them "You have been tried and have not been found wanting..." They had all demonstrated that they could heal themselves and others by their words.

She maintained the Hopkins Associations that she and Mary Plunkett had created. They were support groups for graduates, and included as many of her former students as she could find.

Evolving

Slowly, Emma began to feel that her work was more about being in relationship with God and less about training healers. What she had begun as a healing profession was now a ministry. And, as the nature of Emma's own ministry became clear, one of the members of her board, a Methodist minister, ordained her and empowered her to ordain others.

The years that followed were very productive. Emma ordained 110 ministers, sending them out into the world to "teach the gospel, heal the sick, and cast out passions."

Emma had learned many things from her teacher, Mrs. Eddy, and she applied them in her work. Unlike her teacher, though, Emma never insisted that her students follow only *her* words and *her* understanding. She encouraged all of her students to find their own words and form their own practice—or school, or church— in whatever way they were called by the divine Presence she encouraged them to rely on.

For example, a woman named Mrs. Kate Bingham, from Pueblo, Colorado, wrote and asked to stay with her to address what had been diagnosed as an "incurable" illness. Emma agreed and Mrs. Bingham stayed with her for several weeks, went through her course, and was healed.

Then, when she went home, Mrs. Bingham immediately began teaching others the new way of being, as Emma had instructed. Two members of that class, Nona and Fannie Brooks, were healed in the process, and began their own healing ministry a few years later in Denver, which they called Divine Science.

In another example, one of Emma's first students, E.B. Weeks, delivered a series of classes in Kansas City soon after he graduated. Charles and Myrtle Fillmore, a middle-aged couple with major health issues, attended his first lecture, which was based on Emma's first lesson.

They were healed as a result, and were inspired to share their healing process. They set up the prayer service that's now known as Silent Unity, published their own magazine, and became devoted students of hers. They even named their next son Royal, because of her teachings that we are all the "royal children of the Highest King."

Later, after she ordained them, and with her support and blessing, they created their own Unity church and founded the world-famous Unity Village in Lees Summit, Missouri.[4]

Many small ministries were established around the country during those years, as well.

---

[4] The story of how they did so is in *The Power of Unity: the amazing discoveries of Charles Fillmore*, a Paths of Power book from WiseWoman Press.

Life was more and more filled with good. Emma continued to write a regular Bible study column in the local paper as well as articles in the journal for the Hopkins Association. She studied all the latest books and articles about other religions and science and the new science of Metaphysics. She was invited to speak all over the country, and her ideas became the basis for a metaphysical movement in London, too.

Often, people in the audience were healed simply by listening to her explain the logic behind Jesus' teachings and power. Sometimes people would copy down her lectures in shorthand as she spoke and later type them up for others to read (no tape recorders, then!).[5]

While many of her students were men, Emma associated herself and her work with the women's movement. Like Mrs. Eddy, she felt that she was giving women an opportunity to earn a living that would enhance their own lives, as well. She took this idea much further than Mrs. Eddy, however, and this was shown most clearly at the Great Chicago World's Fair and Exposition of 1893.

---

[5] Some of these are now available as *The Gospel Series, The Judgment Series,* and *Esoteric Philosophy*—all available from WiseWoman Press.

There, Emma placed a booth in the Women's Pavilion, with Jane Addams' settlement house work, and groups that were working for suffrage, fair labor, and temperance. Mrs. Eddy's Church of Christ, Scientist, was on display in the Religions Pavilion among the world's churches and temple traditions.

So Emma's material reached a broad base of women from all over the world, while Mrs. Eddy's church became one of the world's great religious institutions.

Letting Go

Emma refused to create an institution. Once others had formed schools and churches of their own, she let them go with her blessing.

For the next few years, independent Hopkins Associations were thriving all over the country and thousands of people were healing themselves and teaching others to heal as well. They taught from Emma's notes and the copies of her lectures that people shared, but they used their own language and experience as well, which she was glad to see.

Then, in 1895, the Hopkins Association in New Orleans sent a letter to her requesting permission to open a Hopkins Seminary there. It looked to Emma like an answer to prayer: someone else was ready to carry the torch! She immediately agreed and the new Seminary was up and operating that fall.

Then, at the end of that school year, when the New Orleans school was doing well, Emma dissolved the Chicago Seminary.

She was relieved that she would no longer have to maintain an institution or to possess the things necessary to keep it going. Now she could focus her attention on experiencing and sharing God's good, and others could carry the light that she'd tended so carefully.

So, in 1896, Emma sold or gave away everything she had except a single suitcase full of clothes, books, pens, and paper, and began a new life as an itinerant healer and teacher. And, determined to own as little as possible, she lived out of that single suitcase for most of the next twenty-eight years.

On Her Own

The next stage in Emma's life was filled with constant change on the outside, and more and more stillness within. As she devoted more of her time to feeling the Presence in her life, she had less inclination to be around others. So she set up a way of life that made her "time in the Silence" easy.

She spent some time each year living on her mother's farm, where she'd grown up and where her younger sister, Estelle, now lived. Then she spent several weeks or months living in hotels and homes around the U.S. and Europe.

In 1901, her husband, seeing that she was not ever returning to live with him, divorced her and remarried. Several years later she told a friend, "You know I wouldn't look at the best man that ever walked the planet. I am married to God."

For several years she called a hotel suite in New York City her primary home. She spent each winter, and a few summers, in New York. Most days she would stay in her rooms, providing individual healing sessions to some of the most famous, as well as the least-known residents of that city. At one point, she told a friend, there were four people vying for every appointment she could offer.[6] Sometimes she would use her time alone to "send" healing thoughts and energy to someone she didn't have time to see—often with the same results!

In 1917, a woman came to see Emma to be treated for emotional and physical problems. Her name was Mabel Dodge, and she was famous in the New York and Europe for her parties and her support of interesting people. She would visit Emma as many as 3 times a week, lying quietly on a couch while Emma spoke words of truth. Soon she felt so good that she began sending her friends.

Mabel and Emma began to send letters to each other, and some of those were found among Mabel's belongings when she passed on in the 1950s. In those letters, Emma shared some of her feelings about the people she helped, saying "The success of my students is my joy... Like their mother their uplifts hit me harder than my own."

---

[6] The letters between Emma and Mabel Dodge (who became Mrs. Mabel Luhan during this period) have been found in Luhan's papers and are quoted extensively in Gail Harley's *Emma Curtis Hopkins, Forgotten Founder of New Thought*.

Emma shared that she saw the hidden self of all her students: what she called their Holy Essence. She told Mabel that her goal was to get them to see that in themselves, and not get caught up in the small stuff of daily life.

From those letters, we learn that in spring of 1919, Emma went to Taos, New Mexico, for a long visit with Mabel. A number of famous writers and artists lived there then, including Georgia O'Keefe, the painter, and D. H. Lawrence, the writer. Mabel worked and played with all of them and it's likely that Emma met them during her visit.

Emma came home from that visit with sage to cleanse peoples' energy and cornmeal to offer the earth. She had spent time with a Pueblo healer and recognized that there, as well as in the Bible and other spiritual books, Truth was seen and practiced.

Everywhere Emma went she addressed Hopkins Association meetings and worked with individuals. She charged $50 for twelve sessions, which was a lot of money in those days,[7] but it was worth it for the

---

[7] In 1900 a penny bought a loaf of bread; a nickel was good for all day at an amusement park; a dollar was a normal day's pay. Today a loaf of bread costs $2.50 to $4; an amusement park day-pass starts at $20; and minimum wage means a day's work is at least $45.

many who were healed of "incurable" or "terminal" illnesses, or just plain "chronic" complaints.

During these years, Emma came to call her work "high mysticism." She felt that she and her students were connecting with God and letting divine power work in them and through them. In her lessons, she taught people to "look up" to God and "maintain the upward vision." So, at her request, the Hopkins Associations changed their name to the High Watch Fellowship.

Around the same time, her son, now grown and a merchant marine, passed away at sea near Venezuela—which caused her to realize, at a deeper level than ever, that we are never truly separated from those we love.

Over the years, the many churches and study centers that she had helped form had, along with others based on the ideas of Ralph Waldo Emerson and Mrs. Eddy's teacher, Dr. Quimby, become identified as the "New Thought" movement. Several thousand study groups, churches, and centers were involved, and the International New Thought Alliance was formed soon after she closed her seminary.

Emma was nominated for president of the Alliance in 1918, which is still a major organization of New Thought churches. She refused the office, but attended the conference in New York that year, and also published her last writings in a book called *High Mysticism.*

She continued to speak to groups and provide individual treatments for clients for the next several years. In letters to Mabel Lujan, she described what it was like to be able to see a client and then relax, alone, for a while, and experience the delight of God's Presence in her mind, body, soul, and spirit. Sometimes, she said, it felt as if her soul wanted to leave her body to be always in that Presence.

Then a series of heart problems in 1923 made it impossible for her to live alone. Saying that she was experiencing "not so much an illness, but rather God terminating a career,"[8] she spent several months on the family farm with her sister "who," she wrote to Mabel, "takes divine care of me." It was a lovely, quiet time of feeling God's Presence everywhere in her life and world.

The next year, when she was strong enough to travel, she went back to her New York hotel. She felt drawn more and more inward and spent more and more of her

[8] This is from a series of letters quoted extensively in Gail Harley's *Emma Curtis Hopkins, Forgotten Founder of New Thought.*

time focusing on an experience of the Presence within. So she gave up public speaking and reduced her private practice to meetings with a few individual clients in her room.

Among these few was a spiritual seeker who had made quite a reputation as a speaker, but who felt that he hadn't quite got a handle on the essence of the science. His name was Ernest Holmes.

He thought their first meeting would be an interview, but it turned out to be the first of her series of twelve lessons. He quickly rearranged his schedule to allow for this amazing gift.

By the time they were done he had his clarity. Immediately, he sat down to write his own version of these teachings in a book he called, *Science of Mind.*[9]

Soon after meeting with Holmes, Emma went back to the family farm in Connecticut to rest and feel more deeply her connection with God.

The next months were spent quietly on the farm with her sister and occasional visitors.

A few of her students had purchased a farm nearby. They called it High Watch Farm and the women who lived there came frequently to read and share their experiences with her.

One April evening in 1925, Emma called for one of the women from that farm to come read her a few favorite passages from the Bible. While listening, she closed her eyes to feel the Presence more deeply, and let her spirit leave her body forever.

Emma Curtis Hopkins learned how to access the Power to heal and found that it was a power to bring forth all kinds of good in our lives—especially when, as all the

---

[9] Read more about what Ernest Holmes did in *A Power Greater than Magic: the extraordinary life of Ernest Holmes,* a Paths of Power book from WiseWoman Press.

great spiritual teachers have told us, it is shared.

So, today, over a hundred years after she began teaching and writing, thousands of people read her words in books, find her ideas online, or hear her teachings interpreted by teachers and ministers in Unity and Divine Science churches, Centers for Spiritual Living, and Sanctuaries of Truth—and they, too, feel the power of Good working in their lives.

Her Message

Emma said that Jesus taught 12 ideas, which could be found in other spiritual traditions, but only Jesus embodied all of them. Her work and treatments were always to help people experience the higher Truth of Jesus' teachings.

She taught these ideas as 12 lessons. Each time she presented them, she offered different stories and quotes from other religions and the past to help people understand them.

Her first 6 lessons focus on the student's own health and well-being. Emma said these are our life's purpose. Lessons 7-12 help us apply the same principles to others. Emma called this our ministry.

Lesson 1 is that God is all Good and is everywhere present. Since this Good is the only power working in the universe, and since we do everything we do to try to get our good, it shapes our lives, our bodies, and our world.

Lesson 2 is that a lot of our old ideas about God and ourselves get in the way of experiencing God's good in our lives. We don't have to be limited by them, though. We can release and be done with them, in the same way as Jesus turned his back on fear and temptation and went on to fulfill all the prophecies—which was his life's goal, his Good.

Lesson 3 says that when we turn away from ideas that block our experience of God, we open space in our minds and lives to claim or declare more of God's good in our lives. That way we know that we live, move, and have our being in our good.

Lesson 4 is that we can change our experience at any time. We do this by insisting on what we know to be true even if things around us seem to look like what we don't want. Emma called it "Faith," and said it was the "confidence to command." She said that the more we use it the more powerful it is, until, as Jesus said, we can "say to the mountain, 'Move!' and it will move."

Lesson 5 is the power of the spoken, or clearly thought, word. By speaking what we know to be true, and writing down all the ways we see that truth expressed in our world, we increase our experience of God's good in our lives.

Lesson 6 is understanding how Jesus did what he did. By practicing lessons 1-5, one lesson each day, we begin to understand that God's will *is* done "on earth as in heaven," right now.

Lesson 7 shows us how to help someone else know the truth about God's omnipresent good working in their lives. When we see someone who doesn't seem well or happy, we can think or say how wonderful it is that God's life and joy is everywhere, in everyone, and they'll feel better.

Lesson 8 shows us how to help someone else get rid of thoughts and ideas that block their experience of God's good. Emma reminds us not to imagine that anyone is deceiving us, lying to us, or pretending to be anything but their own truly good divine Self—because God's good is in everyone, everywhere.

Lesson 9 shows us how to help someone know that they have all the power they need to be well, whole, and happy. We remember that nobody is ever separated from God's good, which is in and all around everyone, all the time.

Lesson 10 helps us know how we heal ourselves and others. Emma shows us how to teach others to do the same, reminding us never to accuse anyone of not knowing what they need to know or of doing foolish things, because God's wisdom is in everyone, all the time.

Lesson 11 shows us how to see everyone as part of God's essence, doing and being God's good in the world and in our lives. Because we know that only good truly exists, any other appearance is unreal.

Lesson 12 shows us the power of Love lifting each of us outside of our old limitations and into a new way of being. As Jesus was resurrected and became the Christ, and Saul, who persecuted the first Christians became Paul the greatest apostle, so we can "transcend," our past limits.

Emma asked her students to focus on these lessons each day of the week, Monday through Saturday. Sunday was a day to think about God's good in our lives in the morning and to share our deepest thoughts in a letter to someone we might not normally be able to speak to in the afternoon (she didn't expect us to mail the letter).

Her guidelines for living as our highest selves are:

1. Be cheerful under all circumstances; to be cheerful is to be praise-full (and praise is the fastest way to generate Power).

2. Sit down at a certain time every day and write down on paper what your idea of Good is. Write the highest ideas of Good you have...

3. Take two of the 12 lessons and repeat them each day. Spend an hour in the morning thinking about the lessons that focus on you, personally (1-6) and an hour in the afternoon on lessons addressing the people around you and your environment (7-12). (Monday is lessons 1 & 7; Tuesday is 2 & 8, etc.)

4. Meditate (sit quietly and listen for God's wisdom) on the readings and your experiences; act accordingly.

To these guidelines, she added one more: "look up." Emma taught that by focusing on our highest idea of God, we open a channel for more of God's good to flow into us. She encouraged her students, whenever they encountered anything that didn't feel wonderful, or just felt grateful, to focus their imagination on God. She was sure (since she'd seen it demonstrated hundreds of times!), that "looking up" would make us all happier, healthier, and more powerful.

For Emma, we are not "just human." We are God's beloved children, born to be powerful healers and bringers of a wonderful new world. She could see that all the old prophecies about a new kind of world were beginning to come to pass. It would be a world of peace and joy and well-being, filled with God's love and light, and she knew her students would make it happen.

Books by Emma Curtis Hopkins

Class Lessons of 1888 (WiseWoman Press)

Drops of Gold (WiseWoman Press)

Esoteric Philosophy (WiseWoman Press)

The Gospel Series (WiseWoman Press)

High Mysticism (DeVorss & WiseWoman Press)

The Judgment Series in Spiritual Science (WiseWoman Press)

Resumé, practice book for the twelve lessons in high mysticism (WiseWoman Press)

Scientific Christian Mental Practice (DeVorss)

Self Treatments, including the Radiant I AM (WiseWoman Press)

Books about Emma

Unveiling Your Hidden Power—by Ruth L Miller (WiseWoman Press)

Emma Curtis Hopkins, forgotten founder of New Thought—by Gail Harley (Syracuse University Press)

About the Author

Ruth L. Miller is a minister who has written several books about the history of what is called "New Thought" or "metaphysical" religion in America. Her first book, *150 Years of Healing* is an introduction to the founders and leaders of the New Thought movement. Another book, *Unveiling Your Hidden Power,* explains the teachings of Emma Curtis Hopkins, and is published by WiseWoman Press as a text, a workbook, or as a guide for teachers.

Dr. Miller earned degrees in anthropology, cybernetics, environmental studies, and systems science, then worked as a futurist and professor, before preparing for ordination as a minister. In the process, she raised two daughters, one of whom is now a doctor and the other is a media producer. She now serves Unity and Religious Science centers in Oregon, living in a cottage where the forest comes down to the ocean.

About the Illustrator

Martha Shonkwiler is a retired school teacher, perpetual student, and a grandmother. After a career as a teacher, she studied "Healing through Art and Spirituality," receiving three theological seminary and university degrees. Then she volunteered for six years as a chaplain, labyrinth facilitator, art therapist and "Healing Touch" practitioner at the hospital in Grants Pass, Oregon, where she lives in the beautiful woods.

Her focus now is relaxing, creating art, and enjoying her grandchildren (and children) with nature walks, art, and travel adventures. Martha appreciates the Grants Pass Center for Spiritual Living.

WiseWoman Press

1521 N Jantzen Ave #143
Portland, Oregon 97217
800.603.3005
www.wisewomanpress.com

Books by Emma Curtis Hopkins:

- Class Lessons of 1888
- Drops of Gold (a journal)
- Esoteric Philosophy
- The Gospel Series
- High Mysticism
- The Judgment Series
- Resume
- Self Treatments

The Paths of Power Series for young readers:

- A Power Beyond Magic: The Extraordinary Life of Ernest Holmes
- The Power of Unity: The Amazing Discoveries of Charles Fillmore

First Readers' Foundations in Science of Mind:

- Gracie's Adventures with God

Watch our website!

www.wisewomanpress.com

Paths of Power

Boys and girls and men and women all over the world have found a kind of power that transforms lives. These are their stories—how they found the power, what they did with it, and how their own lives were transformed in the process.

This kind of power is greater than magic, because it transforms the person or situation, instead of just changing appearances. And it is, as the teacher Emma Hopkins said, "more than supernatural; it is supremely natural."

The Paths of Power series tells the stories of those who've gone before us so that new generations will discover and use these remarkably human, God-given abilities.